FUTURE UNDERWATER TOMAHAWK

random acts of poetry

by

Ryan Buynak

Future Underwater Tomahawk
Published by:
Coyote Blood Press,
an imprint of
Paradisiac Publishing

Awesome Badass Cover by Ashley Camper
www.ashleycamper.com

ISBN-13:
978-0692673577
ISBN-10:
0692673571

other titles by Ryan Buynak:
Yo Quiero Mas Sangre
The Ghost of the Wooden Squid
Montreal on October

for
ever

Poem

It,
this,
Life...

is just an awesome interval.

It is, indeed, a sad and sorry shame
that someone had to go
and invent an afterlife.

Mix Tape 8 & How to Disappear Completely

2. *Self Portrait* by Balto
3. *Milk* by Kings of Leon
4. *Put It On* by Big L
5. *Anywhere With You* by Saves The Day
6. *Young Glass* (Acoustic Version) by Hey Rosetta!
7. *So What'Cha Want* by Beastie Boys
8. *Something of Love* by Ivy Mairi
9. *54-46 That's My Number* by Toots and The Maytals

*don't worry about #1 or #10

Gnaw the Always

love
is
a pain
in the neck.

New York City
is always under my eyelids.

where you pull me,
your cry,
wears our listening.

my oh my,
how I've grown.

space is needed in outer
and the louder you are
the softer the words.

cum
catch me.

Knock On Your Teeth

To get lazy mean
walking by old earl bosses
along boulevards and broken necks.

Crazy *Nopes* and *Nothings*
call corners exactly corners.

Catch the glamour
by the nod and the noodle
and just be mean,
plain and not simple.

Mean is good and fine and fire gone.

God is mean.
He or she
probably doesn't like you.

He or she definitely
doesn't like me.

Don't be unwanted,
be a lion for a day
and click your fangs
on the lords of steel.

Field Risks

don't take my wild wide world for it,
dear provocateur and door advocate,
as a giraffe coming to some sort of realization,
you should know when to steal
the days away from change.
just as seasons begin to spit and split,
burn yourself unto mind
by time, and aside from a scotch ale in the shower,
this line will be a moment and a minute,
long drawing shall we be.
bleeding blood and dreaming dreams,
I never try to,
but it's all been done before,
before me and before you,
before borne truth and prescience.
left of stress while east of rivers,
cause and effect, and cause and affect,
when there is nothing, there is something,
field risks and goodnights,
captured by wild writings and lunar haunts.
a month and a day,
a day and a month, trembling after noons
and a space betraying in between,
trusts the tusks to be tough
back to the beginning of poems in place.

Practice the Art of Axe Throwing

I am not normal,
not here,
not anywhere,
and
these werds,
however misspelled,
are blades
meant to be thrown
at the wide world,
directly.

as brown as leaves can get,
sleep is what you should.

so go
hickory and/or orange American
only because of the umbrellas
carrying
the vibrant mix.

just eat and repeat and watch TBS.
I wish my ankle
would just go the way of the buffalo.
there will be no more stories for your middle.
I like when you type my name
unto the internet.

be a piano, mon cher,
be the beautiful bastard Autumn
and all the summers that it took.

I wish my middle name were Spectacular.
yes, it is just Marcel, for real.
and on that great note,
I am going to limp my way to the forest
for food.

I haven't been through
what you've been through
and we can use that as an excuse...

or
better yet,
Practice the art of hatchet catching.

Not Even the Sun

The greatest sum
of anything
in the wide world
is probably pain.

Not even the sun
is immune from death.

A girl's JV basketball team
lives and loses,
somewhere.

Think about it.

I Feel Time Tick Away
in My Bastard Blood Cells

If you crush wise old Novembers
and head into life for whatever reason
while simply ignoring windows,
you will just be a sauce, just sitting in a busy diner.

I name the stars after your shoulders,
and the same things make you wide-eyed and wild.

Let's see what hides inside;
she was lost amongst the noise and laughs and life's
casual dying.
This is a gold mine of mine.

Cockamamie

and the next thing I know,
Frank and I are in a junkyard
looking for the front end of a Dodge.

my pants are ripped and my
mustache is bloody,
but the weird thing is,
of a sudden,
we had a dog with us,
a gentle German Shepard;
from where it came I have no sniffing idea.

then the police came
with their German Sheps,
and asked us for our signatures.
and I, for some reason,
thought of Kyle,
and noticed that the moon
was already visible in the Florida day;
it was close to being full or empty.

Frank put it best
when he said you
can't plan on parts.

He was talking about car parts,
but I thought of Life parts.

Those words keep me on my feet

when drunk under sober moons,
and when life seems like it will fall apart.

Burn Into Vision

I□ dabble.□

I am just a person who likes to dabble in stories.
a liar, if you will.
the fact that I write them down some how makes it a
sad vocation.

this might be a lie:
re-runs of *Cheers*.

Medicinal brunette
to keep the heart going,
ignorantly.

this might be true:
brunch, bottoms up.

movies, make-believe.
and minus memories, much madness.
don't believe everything
that you read.
this is no laughing matter.

you're father was right, you are a pussy.

This End Up

Sweating and starving in Brooklyn,
and staring across the stars that sit on nicks
on shoulders of women I've loved so long...

Must've lost eight and a half pounds
just from living in four days' heat,
as opposed to one or three, the best is me.

Memories return like Honda Civics,
but they disappear like Southern California
motorcycles.

You have nothing to fear,
as long as your wayward dreams still think you are
young.

I carry empty hands
in case of catching rain,
or collecting you.

Moon, Over Easy

yellow yellow yes.
in the key of sea.

I don't make the rules.
and I'm glad I do not.

gravity is a hot spot.
 while I like to sit on top of televisions.
in a motive song.
ten cuddlings shy.

my pistol should prove proof.
bullets are me.
and knives are you.

I will buy you breakfast.
for dinner.

A Poem Called A Poem for Yes

used to work in a food truck.
listened to folk music.
as loud as one can listen to sad bastard music.
after one, or two, or eleven and a half cocktails.
spilled half of number seven on my shoes.
it's not whiskey, it's a time machine.
with two days at the zoo.
will bring you water balloon fires.
the Bowery Ballroom had me last night.
gripped in scissors.
and epic.
used to work for an Israeli newspaper.
layout and layoffs.
and smiles and frowns.
a thousand songs are in there somewhere.
and other tiny things.
trading time for pockets full of minutes.
and moments.
going next to the Colorado regrets.
and Devil birthdays.
that keep coming.
everything.
was nothing.
but the world and a heart.
ending.
eventually.
probably on a morning quite like this morning.
with rain and bad news bears.
for yes.
but the world and a human heart that has stopped

working.
celestial in the way of affect.
from the first time eyes blink life.
slowly starting relative time.
and food jobs and a billion books.
living the dash on the face of tombstone fun.

Thank You, 2011 and 2012, Respectively

You delivered strength and wrath
like a pizza delivery boy
in Central Florida.

And you topped it off
with a terrific January
of lost jobs and heart attacks.

Thanks for the days in those years
for making me wiser,
and for disappearing ever so swiftly.

No Rhymes

no traffic, so I go.
no jam for my breakfast toast.
twenty minutes ago.
the black pavement moans.

Murderee, I miss your shoulder stars the most.

so very listless listless listless...
so sad in modern Rome.

the host of the hill.
the ghost of the heart.

we rose from the ground.
as the days go by.
We wonder why.

don't hang your heart on things like love.

Conversation, There Is So Much Left

to say...

what's up, Cut?
what's up, Mud?

Hit me up on the hip.

just worked the night away at a cocktail lounge in
White Harlem.
just the same as your life in Silver Lake or Winter Park
or Istanbul.

walk it off now.
we can tell the world now
how it feels to be...
nevermind.

Every beast for himself.
Live with the Lions
or live with the snakes and the rats.

call me up on the telephone
and I will say
to watch where you kick your feet.

I heard her laugh.
once.

thanks, Step-Nasty.
Your father screams:

what's next for the Ray?

writing and travel.

my life is good and simple.
shoot me to the ground.

Main Street at Cinnamon Crossing

Gunnysacks.
Lizards.
Yellow mistress.

Teeth.
As old statues.
I miss that old orange tree,
the one with the biting snails.

I don't want to be victory.

Miami sorrows
be repeated,
and be alive;
and her round face is the world to me.

Right click
the scenery as it passes our car window.

Pugilist

sometimes
something's gotta give
and I'm the one to give it.

Give it to the burn.
Give it to the streets.
Give it to the wheels
that desire your feet.

I want to be incapable
of remorse.
a hat is all that I have.
my greatest talent
is the ability to disappoint.

Fang Sky

thunder rattles the big windows,
outside of which the palms trees bend
in the wind.

my thumbs break with the best
in this house we call Vacation.

I turn the television off and turn to my tiger,
a book of lovely thieves,
stealing my minutes.

grey approaches from the south,
killing the blue afternoon.
this is the place Hashem finds
me happy.

I sit with vodka and wait for the
cadence of rain.
it starts slowly and grows into a
rattle of symbols with many
syllables.

my eyes are dry, my heart is full;
I hear her voice calling my name
through the lightning.

What's New, Pussycat?

(for Hiten)

Want to listen to British mod
music in the sad bastard afternoon
and pretend everything's just fine?

Want to get some blow
and destroy the next three afternoons,
and our subsequent miniscule bank accounts?

What do you honk?
While I think about going to Montreal.
Forever.

This Belgian IPA
in front of me
has a lot of bite to it,
peppery,
orange zest,
a glass of last minute regret
on a night of last minute regret.

Okay, fair enough,
I will find out how to forget
for two Junes and an extra August.
I'm sorry, Shy Shy.
To this day, I swear I was nice,
but I was not,
not even ready
to be.
Me.

Sometimes We Glide

Sometimes we glide
and sing sad love songs
to stone sideways.

Count your teeth with your tongue
and just be with me.

I try not to
show.
Fear.
I run around this town
like nothing matters.

I sweat on subways and see yellow violets,
with hipsters with Arcade Fire shirts,
writing poetry on the Rumbler.

I am nostalgic for a time that never really existed.

Escape.
Learn with me slowly.

twelve minute songs

I make up these whispers.

If it's not one thing,
it's another.

no wonder.

we wish for moments
in which we say, absently,
"t his is kinda fun."

But it kills us.

I cover my loose teeth
with smoke and violins;
darling, I ain't sorry
for rosewood and idiots.

a man can't control his dreams.

Poem

I threw our microwave into the river.
No thank on that, I said.
Thank the pianos.
For playing.
I'll just order delivery forever.
Good riddance.
Only forks and exclamation points
are in my ever kitchen.
And one hammer, near the window point-of-view.

In case of emergency, break class.

Alex

That ground that surrounds your feet
is worth worshipping.

What is it like
being the most beautiful gal in the whole goddamn
world?

I'd follow you through cottonfields,
and back in time.
I'd follow you through blackberry bushes
and into the future.

You broadcast whispers
to the rain.
Be my sword
and I will gladly be your fool.

Come back to bed.
Be you.
I was just thinkin' and hopin'.
Just think about it.

Kickstand

I have a pal.
just over Raleigh hill.
he is a detective.

I ride a borrowed bike there.
to say goodbye.

his wife answers the door.
says he is not home.
double homicide.

murder happens in every neighborhood.

I give her a CD to give to him.
she does not like me.
says I am a bad influence.
she is right.

later that evening.
I pack my bags.
just a bunch of clothes and bullshit.

dinner and cigarettes.
beer, bourbon, and a bridge.

I can hear the east coast saying 'don't you frown,
goddamn it.'

I give the bike back, goodbye for now.

I drink a beer.
mop the floor.
and I do the last of tonight's life's dirty dishes.

The Process of Getting to Bed-Stuy

no go.
relieved.
I am on your side.
only for a while, of course.
pissing down in the Essex stop on the line.
I've been living in applauded tension.
I have been living in funny bone elbows.
for four hours, plus a few weak weeks.
eating canned corn.
writing about other foods for other people.
burning blue sweaters.
sitting in palace grin.
sleeping in cottage doors.
the Rumbler and Marcus Garvey Blvd.
new things in my money or lack thereof.
at least there is a garden.
and an Italian and a Jongo.
you'll see.
I've been living in a let.
I've been dying in a window.
grand. the bed. my eyelids.
I've been living amongst the mornings.
right now the world only has my feet.
I have to make my own patience.
I use my shoulders and her stars.
our sorrows repeated be.
well, I still mean nothing.
however, I once made a bird feeder.

Letter Letters

I love that pink sky you sent.
It was daughter perfect.
Thanks for sending it my way.
Indeed, tomorrow is eventual.

Beauty and chaos and adventure.
all three have my attention.
during these long lost afternoons.
brought to us by mac-n-cheese and existence.

I take my hat off.
tickle the fear.
and listen to typing fingers.
this is the alphabet in New Amsterdam.

here and now and now and here.
everything is different, my foot on the gas.
Fridays will never just be Fridays anymore.

Hashem even made the goddamn post office good.

Iris in the End

never made to win.

the lake departed,
and in the creek we are forgotten.

it's difficult not to give up
after such a bloody battle.

take the cap off the bottle
and
leave her body in the snow...
bracelets still on her wrist.

+Jazzbrunch

with good guns
and a bloody mary or three
in a slow-spinning vestibule
with chairs made of wicker
and wood,
and accidental great whites
smiling from the ceiling,
music slips in from her viola tongue.

we wish we were in a class
of language
by Fridays and last night's
setting fire to station wagons,
knowing not how to prevail
from our separate young boats;
one last sip,
we watch the sunrise
and we let life be the same,
equal distance between our names.

the afternoon ends with abnormal thunder
walking overhead like dead neighbors.

on the ground we walk their way, too.
so this is Rhode Island?
then music slips in.
again.

Poem

The name of this book
was going to be *Air Mattress Sex*,
but then my Editor and Publisher
made me change it.

kitchens [cause] women

slept on the street
on a Montreal morning.
best soundtrack snooze I ever had.
then I snuck into an American movie
and slept in there, too.
subsequently, found laughter.
got lost in some places I've been before.
I hit the day in the elbow with a Kaiser blade.
suspended, the hits were near the trees.
my life is so far away from me.
at least the Oldsmobile sky
is still above me.
I am rearviewmirrors.
I am going to LA tomorrow.
don't waste your time with long division
in the kitchen.

I am going to cook up a doozy
of a movie, myself.

Lines in the Sky, part 1

imagine flying, impossibly.

she is left handed.
she is polite.

there is something wrong with me.

I laugh at the end of it all.

Lines in the Sky, part 2

urgent and deeply,
I breathe at an open window,
having just learned news
of the early movement of nothing.

we will sleep in the same bed again.

constellation aftermath,
her ribs, her brilliant father,
pop music, etc.

Still Life with Fast Food

silly scars
dot the landscape
like lonely lighthouses
with orange spiral staircases
leading all the way to a land
of dinosaur hair, and heaven.

it's funny.

like nowadays
when you tell your friends
you just ate McDonald's,
and they look at you like you are insane
or retarded or suicidal.
Maybe. All. Three.

eyebrows,
and a painted smile,
like a calm cattail pond,
drip off the canvas
with a grin.

this is him.

the future shoulders
not with stars or nicks,
but pulpits on which to beg
for forgiveness from
fun performers on legs.

birds fly and swoop down.
this is happening now.

a kite already on the skids,
dialing phones and ignoring.
this is bliss.
it is supposed to exist.
just eat and live.

Bewail You

I don't think I ever loved you,
        but the world is dying to meet you.

Lunch

I woke with a new headache,
a new pimple, and someone else's sweatshirt.

surprised by the destruction of memories,
a good job drunk on my part,
also, surprised by the meatball appetite,
I put on sunglasses and shoes,
and cursed the day for being so nice.

sadness is supposed to be reserved
for thunderstorms and soup.

I got a Five-Dollar Footlong from Subway,
and ended up giving half to a young hobo with a dog.
He gave half of the half to his mutt.
He said his name was Harold.
I sat with this fellow for a quiet hour.
We spoke of the nice weather.

Before heading off to look for a job,
I asked Harold his favorite
Red Hot Chili Peppers song
and he responded
without hesitation,
"*Soul to Squeeze*, man!
    That jam was on the Coneheads soundtrack!"

$140 of Weirdness

how many cemeteries were flooded
for your little lake of love?

well, when wearing a weird hat
I must get weird.
and since you've read this far,
I will keep polluting this river.
far be it from me to deny
the catfish their deserved demise.
I love alliteration, obviously,
and I love you.

trust me, *Murcielaga*, I struggle.

the rain just won a hundred and forty bucks on a bet.

trust me, stars, I write.

the underwater landscape is different here.

trust me, treble clef, I want.

the edges of the pages are frayed
but still readable
and this Canadian vodka
tastes like salt water.

persistence and determination
are alone omnipotent, mud.

Pointedly Me, Mercy, Motherfuckers

I love that you motherfuckers think
you're better than me,
that I need help.
yours, especially.

we are all degenerates.
we are all evil;
some folks just justify it all
in a different way.

you paper toilets!
I don't need to be addicted
to your sinew or your tin sheep.
and I don't need your wayward advice;
I can buy my own alkaloids.

then.
one day.
9mm slug shot to the back.
and BLAM!!!
my heart will leave my chest for the sidewalk.

and thanks for the mistakes, Heart of Hearts,
I fucking followed you everywhere
(and no one can take that away from me).

Plenty

Do me a favor,
and don't ever apologize to me.

Ever.

Why, you ask,
well,
 because you never need to.

I am sure
I am far worse a person
than you'll ever be.

This is the wind,
and it is my fault
for blowing your pointless
umbrella up Third Ave.

Selected

I am going to show you what it takes
to get out alive
from one of the toughest places on Earth.

this is a place where light eats spiders.
this is a place in which knives come alive.
this is a place where things happen before they ever
happen.

the course is rough and rugged.
crocodiles might eat your hearts.
and from which no one comes back.

bring a bunch of socks and a lunch
and a heavy heart and hard shoulders with stars on
them,
and a little luck and a drawbridge,
because
you have been selected to fall in
love.

there is no escaping this shit.

My Leg is Bleeding

every record.
florist apprentice.
also waiting tables.
in the belly of a billy goat.
that living room.
one criminal and a few nurses
into one afternoon.
the biscuits are on your side.
drinkin' in the hot shotgun seat.
damn you.
I can't wait to kill you
and steal your car.

Kevin Costner

this is something...

and I am far, far away
with a future yawning,
arms letting go,
telling stories of our
possible lives,
and having all the sarcastic fun.

dim porch light
barnacled in the distance
on an onion roof,
I find my place
amongst the bugs...

we are all longing to be free
but we can't help it,
we are addicted to light.

act like you've been here before.

sing from the West,
and let's waste some money...

I know my place
among the flowers in the rubbish;
I sing there, too.

get the angles right,
for tomorrow is as alive as death,

just like a photograph.
now I recognize
that you were there,
and so was I.

rest your legs.

Knitting Nothing

sorry, Mr. Percy.
I say on a Sunday.
got stuck invisible as life.
on 29th street.
invisible as my hand.
which I see everyday.
ignore.
continue.
I come alight on 33rd and Park.
walk.
in the biggest rooms we die.
adios, Mr. Percy.
the loud librarian is now as good as dead.
lost in his automobile.
probably just another fender on 57th street.
coughing into life.
the search starts.
and should never end.
What is it you seek - God? you ask with a smile.
no.

Atelier

I am playing backgammon.
in symphonies.
New Year's eve.
Montreal middle midnight.

we laugh.
in workshops.
and under fireworks.
I don't know anyone's name here.

walking be game.
lost in another film.
cold wind whipping through my naked tattoos.

I am a man who never...

Monday's train.
will not be the same.
I am in the middle of truth.
war silver.

I have come from the kitchen.
of the sun.
And, oh, how I write.
through the sky.

I take a bath.
It's snowing in this plastic place.
and we are dancing in free dreams.
for a small price.

Once Upon a Time...
There Was a Pineapple
and a Tomahawk

I am a bad person in love with bad people.
Blockbuster Video bullshit, a sea of whiskey.
I fight problems with problems,
but I wear a watch.

There is something
I have been meaning to tell you.
But I will wait.
This is not the venue for such discussions.

The radio is playing our songs.
I am eating beer and drinking cheese.
Los Angeles is calling, edits,
and I miss Montreal.

This isn't who I am.
from confidence to self-doubt.
in one hundred and sixty two seconds.
I am trying to wear hats.

I'm not larger than life.

black sky basement tapes

like a renegade
with hearts
where her
eyes should be,
beating with blinks,
eyes distressed in open chest.

fists like feathers.
fists like parenthetical lions.
fists like goodbyes.
fists in in-between doors.
fists like etc.

Duchess

I will say
I am so afraid
how this twisted train
will come to its inevitable end.

We bonded over books and broken bones.

the world is waiting, too,
while I piss in your hand,
and someone is French-kissing someone else;
just as well, someone else is making a collage of it all.

so then we grew up.

I still know nothing,
and
in the end it boils down to accountability.
I have none so I will die with the shoes on my feet.

don't be sad, Duchess.
don't be angry.
drink a glass of wine and take a nap and dream of me.
I'm was always so demanding,
but I believe in this carnivorous, anti-poetic life.

Living...
I am not good at it, but I love dancing,
here.

How many days do we have left

to do the things that make our hearts speed up?

Let's share donuts anytime.

I want to be a florist and learn the piano.
I want to kiss you hard in the pouring rain just so
you'll shut up.

Sleepy Fire

ten cents of sleepy fire
for the hurry timing of dreaming on earlier said
riverboat:
autoharped, rewarded, black-eyed, felled.
that's just the start of the sawgrass brush.
the bridge is closed...no more wishes, my dear.
the rain has gone away.
the western sky is late.
but if you're gonna die young.
what's the worry with mishap?
might as well be a giraffe riding a bike.
while towing a mini-lion on the handlebars.
that's the best way to disappear, my dear.
the port water has the world painted upside down.
wonder if that is a reflection of here or a different
world entirely?
one in which we don't starve in the middle of all of it
and us in the middle of a thousand raw potatoes.
wow to trucks.
wow to love.

Johnson!

Johnson is pink.
A happy little prick.
Every teller at the bank hates him.
Every drunkard at the bar loves him.

Johnson is a good singer.
An awful lawyer.
An Alabama wonder.
Prankster archetype.

The terror of Owen's Family Funeral Home.
He burned it down last year.
Saying he was cremating the building.
He spent only three weeks in county.

At barely thirty-one.
He is a smooth talker.
A terrible dresser.
A big fan of the band Thin Lizzy.

Johnson doesn't whistle when he walks with his wife.
Johnson's wife, Julie, is jolly.
She broke her hip during childbirth.
Their son is named Windmill Once.
Johnson has a few bullet wounds.
No one knows where Johnson and his wife are from.
They ain't from here.
This small town.

Johnson whistles when he walks alone.

And while he drinks whiskey.
And he does both of those things when he writes.
Goddamn poetry.

A Lot Like Bus Depots

confidence is half the key
and alcohol is the other half...
on nights after a restaurant's life,
and, as they say, we are all just hummin' in the rain.

another battle is won and lost
when ten hipsters risk the Rumbler
for hutch and yak.
fuck Brooklyn.

uptown, don't talk to me about money,
smile for the midnight game of darts,
desolate in spirit and Biddy's is dangerous,
but we all live to die
so who cares if we go poor.

hope is not lost.
I am an airport
and I look like a desk.

A Mexican,
a Marine,
and a Poet
Walk Into a Bar

present tense is all we need,
and less yesterdays.

hanging out after work.
Sawtooth Ale and surprises.
I wanted to go home and write
but good times, great people,
and drinking
took precedent.

we kept saying,
brother,
pour me another,
cut me one more.
midnight came and went.

until.
we closed the wine bar
and walked north,
a Mexican, a U.S. Marine and a poet,
pantomiming tales,
talking about our worlds before this place,
and our girls.

the rain started a bit
and we made our way to danger,

to Biddy's, the Auction House.
The Scotsman was tending the bar,
The Daniel was there with whiskey in hand.

Sure, we took whiskey, too.
Too much.
Sure night of simple grievances,
sure night of laughter,
proving that humans hold adventurous life very close
to hollowed heart,
even if we don't speak the same language.
spring closes in,
as does tomorrow morning,
and we closed the tab with a good night joke
and a punchline of cigarettes,
only no one has a goddamned lighter.

unfinished sympathy 2

three jobs.
plus literature.

three phonecalls.
plus gorgeous.

rain plus bugs in hallways.
Angie plus America plus America.

it's hard to make moments last.
it's hard to keep the dreams you had.

guitars plus drugs.
friends plus friends.

bus plus hill plus commute downtown.
booze plus pills.

stolen books.
plus the Yankees beat the Mariners.

I scratch my beard.
isn't that so?

symphony plus park.
sun plus dark.

playgrounds plus blues.
concrete plus teeth.

awesome swords.
plus the toilet.

I see the big sky in your words.
and I can't forgive it for being so goddamn great.

thanks, kiddo.
plus forever.

page 32 or 67.
plus the sound of watching clouds.
they roll by on an endless sky.

Two Weeks Notice

I quit.
mattresses.
for French Toast and sausage.
and the first coffee.
I quit business hours.
those see-saw moments on corners.
near Mexican bike shop.
across from skinny glasses and nice legs.
I quit the avenue for a boulevard.
the morning quit chilly, skipped.
afternoons quit evenings immediately.
life quits for death.
I quit.
the day at Lake TV.
for a frozen freight train.
I quit.
rivers for rain.
it's all better than waiting so long, indeed.

Petrichor Park

be leave. real leaf.

symphony silence.
a city of sounds blocked out by green and grey sights.
a beautiful old television show playing muddy for me.
without audible weak day weekday weaponry.

the city busses are much nicer out west.
not too crowded, still efficient, green as far as the
environment goes.
tapping in rhythmic brakes up and down hills.

I took a bus there.
to the place where it always smells
like it is just about to rain.
or it just has
(But whenever I go there water is never actually falling
from the sky).

the gnats and the pigeons have all left recently.
only the elderly red-breasted robins remain.
renting worms from the soil.
oblivious to me.
I read a few chapters of a novella called 'Lucinella'.
under an old tree.
I'd like to call it an Oak.
but in truth I don't know what the hell.

I flag the tiny trees with used neckties stolen from
thrift shops.

dressing their trunks up like businessmen.
I even put a blazer on one tree once.
it had arms like a David.

my new shoes got mad muddy.
holy mud will find its way back to my room-to-rent.
there is so much silence.
like this place's volume has been turned down.
so love low.
I take off my top hat and drink some whiskey.
soon, the leaves tell me to leave.
I find the fountain compass,
goodbye another Tuesday, and go.
low and behold, the bus chariot is tick-tocking for an
hour.
just for my day.

This Long Storm

this short poem...
inverted in the kitchen
just vain.

life is worth much more than gold.

scene at two fifteen,
ask the knife,
she replied.
I did spy a ghost joke.

morning candle light,
my cereal without milk,
I want to make you breakfast
for the first time.

desmond sidewalk,
honk horns and get fined by ahead of truth.

windows and tigers,
my friends have flesh in the wind.

tell me it's good to be back.
each morrow.

I think about memories, but not memories.
whisk many.
I am bright on page seventy-one.
we always want.
but we'll never get.

Mine

Montreal Mondays
and NYC Wednesdays
have my silent harp
hidden.

And my hearse.
And the songs that call them themselves mine.
And yours.

I sleep all day.
Because I lay awake.
Counseling the ceiling.
Trying to be funny.

At night.

I wish you still found me interesting.
In the danger.
Drawing near.

I Made These Curtains

I grow silly-style bored of the characters
in the book on this train lift.
I want to write about the characters
in my primeval comedy.
the lovely morose dance through the blue night all
the way to rose mornings,
with fits and feet and appetite and
death, always death around the
corner,
but which corner?
it's unreliable until this cool story.
pigeons don't think about these things.
on the train lift waiting for the framed day.
who knows what they will say on walls.
breakfast for dinner, tall.
on the swollen patio just east of Maple Ave.
a modern day scarecrow.
with a favorite song.
thrown off the bus.
now reading about bounce wrecks.
while farting in a rocking chair.
And I don't care,
I just need ya here.

Fleep Flop

Friends in real life...
What is this, 1996?
Cute little legs.
Crossing streets
In cut-off jean shorts.

And I love ya.
In an instant.
An instant is immeasurable.
Pour a little soap.
And wash my simple hands.

vagabont anti

the rain had ceased.
I went for a walk.
it was just past midnight.
summer had just arrived here,
in this part of the world.
but this night was still cool and the city calm.
I went into a pub and ordered a scotch and milk.
I read an old Pennysaver.
I tried to smile my way into a pretty brunette.
but she stuck to her white wine.
she had big brown eyes.
I wondered what she was about.
same as the rest of them, probably.
crazy and starving for real love.
I left and took the long way home.
along the river.
I stole a bottle of beer from the common grocer.
I meant to drink it on the stoop and get some writing
done.
but I fumbled it and shattered it on concrete steps.
karma doesn't exist.
I opened up my hands.
then the rain came blowing back against windows.

Arkansas Supper

(co-written with Eric Schmidt)

Little Rock is for dirt merchants,
no lie.
white zin with Aunt Linda.
we watch re-runs of *Rosanne,*
and boil our feet.
rubber jerks stop by for a whistle jug.
moonshine eyes in broken hearts.
mother slaps some sense
into my jawbone.
we laugh like asses.
all jobless,
sneezing without bless-you's.
we've got the right ideas for a bloodbath,
but short on execution.
no thank on that..
it is a flawed expression of displeasure.
half a mile from the county fair□
lies Grandma Billy.
I hope the thunder leaves her ghost alone.
pile in the jeep, losers.
it's dinner time.
dry off.

Poem

Act like you've been here before.
With blue lights running down your musical cheeks.
Getting off an hour late.
Getting old.

out in my maybe

pickin' the disbelief outta my teeth.
where'd you get that shiner?

New York, Earth, here.

A yesterday fist.

the walls.
closing in.
with mesh curtains.
and love made for the lights.
and kissing cheeks.

guessing roads.
sounds of songs.
maybe it is bricks and mortar now.
I don't want anyone or anything to shake us away.

who mapped oblivion?
the peacock.
the pineapple.
the tomahawk.

Red Lobster is still here.
like a fateful banner in changing minds.
lawn grass on this world.
connecting to suicide barstools.
carry. banner.

I figure we might move.

up.
taking this love down with me.

we make noise in our generation.
stereos and car windows.
scarves in summer with winter wanting to kill you.

squash city.
don't ask for cigarettes.
she will never ask anything of you.

it's better to feel pain.
than nothing at all.

pay attention, love loser.
I am on your stoop.
screaming about sex and jack-o-lanterns.
and the beginning of the world.
and the last song of last night.

zoo squad

five cents for glory.
the four statue jollyhops have martial bones.
with cotton candy marrow in them.
they are from across the wishing bridge.
with forecasts so damning that laughter makes it
subside.
these four or eight or six folks are forgotten.
can you see me now?
love is not forgotten in two hearts.
east and west.
retired and repaired and beginning to cry life.
let's sell this burning pocket of sugar.
apologies are right across the street.
I promise.
mashed potatoes and gravy fights for us.
we are going to push the dynamite handle down.
nothing is nothing to someone special on precious
sidewalks.

The Calculating Genius of Outrage and Sorrow, Volume 2

To everything
there is a season
and all seasons
end.

My heartbeat
sounds like people
walking down stairs.

Poem

hot boiled Sprite.

I'm with the haunted.

whiskey white curtains.

I like to write about people in airports.

monsters or regular humans?

cool sentences come from her aperture.

everything is going to be okay.

there is no music, but music is on.

respecting a river.

a sloth is your boss.

plagiarize your fasces.

catch up to innocent weather.

God died in his sleep.

heart transplant

dust my weather
with disaster.
I will try to be gone,
but not forever.

would be rich,
what with gold vital organs,
and if I harvest them
I die.

midnight never comes for me,
and this whole place is dark.
I just wonder who you are.
this is my farewell submission.

I feel your ghost
breathing down my shoulders.
I will try to be gone,
but not forever.

the bitch of it all
is all we can do is try.
the real bitch of it all
is we can't ever get it right.

A Pat Part

my Mom loved Barbara Streisand ,
and M.A.S.H.,
the tv show, not the movie...

oh, and yellowish rocks of crack cocaine
and Black Velvet whiskey.

My mom loved the month of March,
I do not know why,
her birthday was in October.

She was born on Friday the 13th.
She held fast to a hand-me-down hutch.
She held a gun to my head once.

Poem

But what else can we do?
Get jobs in offices
and watch the evening news?
That's *one* option.

Part Two Twelve Surrender

Sadness shouldn't begin on a morning so bright,
instead it shall better be suited for gloom
and light rain, not heavy rain,
just a constant drizzle, and a few thunders.

It is this that distinguishes times
in which we are needling change.

You mustn't care about me anymore.

Hope against hope that your night shines
like London street lamps
back in 1936, when we were being borne into
another life.

I meant Czech origins, I meant death.

I just made the world's worst mistake
a human can make.
I need a let down.
I need a bath.
I need a death.

There have been tidal waves
that we have missed,
besides barely rattling our teeth.

This kind of misery is what I call home.
No no no!

How long can you take me and my missteps
and my bullshit,
which happens to glow and feed romance's death?

I know what I want.

The best short story ever written is not like this,
and a man named Breece did not write it.

Downfall or redeeming grace.
Obsessed with colors that mix yellow and red.
Orange shadows over me.
I hate the color orange.

I'll tell you this story in person about a person filing
regret and mistakes in the same folder as mistrust and
misguidance, and love and loss and more regrets and
dodo birds.

So how can someone punch someone
in the gut
and break their heart at the same time?

I am not a force, for this is not love,
after all,
and I never thought it could happen again.

I was the one who stole the manholes all around the
city and sold them for bread.

Hurricane Tongue

The Century Sun With or Without Rain,
don't count the
turned upside down
leaves
of trees
when it rains
like the end
here or there;
and do not,
under any
pasta goodness
circumstances
give up
or go to hell.

go back to the rooftop
with ironic graffiti
and lost love
and fireworks
and Dylan soundtrack(s).

I matter, too, Silver.
Stay gold, Somewhere,
you Gorgeous Fire,
don't forget me.
I set the sun to wake you up.
Forever.

Sugarcane

I see paranormal lights
out of the corner of my right eye,
as I type this sentence
and drink this well whiskey.

A black/white star,
a crime,
nuclear take-your-time's.

Tell me what it's like to be back, goddamn ghost!

I shake.
My coffee is now cold.
It is from this morning.

Spend all our Sundays
in a death row.
Bathroom sunrise sparks
major in the underbed.

We fight as Gut Teeth
and chainsaws and sugarcane
and hammers and windows and exclamation points
and windows
and forks and sing-alongs
and yarn from the island.

We will always be Newlyweds,
somewhere, in time.

The Parsonage

2 cigs.
Chapped lips.
Tin Can.
Matthew Dickman poems and my mustache.
We are the Hipster Generation.

God will end all Kingdoms.
So says the Orca.
the Owl.
Keys to apartments.
We disappear so well.

Google Earth.
Her house in Colorado.
Brooklyn complains.
And during the days.
We decide our favorite animals.

Be my date to the film festival thing,
I say.
Then.
Be a memory.

Poem

We believed above
the Econlockhatchee River!
I only met your father once.

We were better
than that Volkswagen,
the one that I wrecked towards the end.

Part Two Twelve Contender

Twenty-two,
count it,
twenty-two,
broken hearts
within everyheartbeatonthisstreet
fucking beating and fucking,
and among the flashback kids in the backyard
doing keg stands.

Twenty-three if you're counting me,
and there are words we left behind,
33.

A million stories,
different apples
for me to eat like poetry...

and my main morning
woke up angry...

yesterday-today, with vodka,
in a land with bashful burning bushes that aren't
meaning,
no,
they just smoke in the dark.

Thirty-one days in August,
not one with a telephone call.
Eating pizza almost every night for dinner.
The New Yorker only publishes

poetry for old ladies
and kindling firewood.

One summer somewhere
gone forever,
bequeathed golden ghosts
in my heart's heartbeats,
and misunderstood memories.

the good goddamned forest
in my heart
is ready for fire, too.

Thirty-one goodbyes time two,
to money and kids,
always pounding stories
always pouring wine and lies.

Tomorrow

Tomorrow,
Butch, Vernon, and Garfield,
let's go to Brooklyn!

I know a girl in Greenpoint.
She has booze and drugs and food.
She knows the shape we're in.

She says she loves me
and I think I believe her.
I like her eyes a lot and hate her tattoos.

We'll call her in the morning
time, we'll take the L train
and walk the rest.

Don't any of you bastards without saints
try anything with her,
I think I love her, too.

Poem

By the very end,
after the soul grows twice as old,
I will have died
one hundred and sixty two times...

So far, as of today,
I have only died twice;
one hundred and forty-eight
to go.

Or is it twelve rather?
That memory of mine
keeps resetting
itself.

He Wrote, I'm Broken

Hey,
Hola,
hello,
howdy!

one time
tomahawk,
one time
rosebud,
live on,
forgive me,
cut out my tongue.

I love you more than photosynthesis loves the sun.

I'll climb
 on top of you.

I want to sleep
 under your eyelids
or
between your legs.
I want to be your car accident.
I want to be something you'll never forget.

 I miss your smell,
it suited my senses so well.

There is no backing out,
not now.

It Doesn't Hurt As Bad
As I Had Hoped

broke my left wrist in a fall
from grace and ladders.
yes, last night walks under
my father's son's son's head like a train.

burned down the house
before I left for the pub,
stopped at McDonald's first
but not to eat, just watch.

don't feel much like writing today.
there is nothing left of last winter.
there is nothing left of last year.
just a stone and some medicine.

going into the future,
minding my own business.
I am dumb but not stupid
and I still believe in you.

it's the hollow month of November
of the foul year of 2010,
and a heart will eventually return to my chest.
you are a star in my sky, my breast,
I am a citrus bastard.

I will meet you somewhere
in the middle and tell you everything.
Want to go on a date then?

I killed the stage in Montreal.

Now know.
Now no.

She's so angry on the same train,
Hipster Monday,
Yacht rock X-mas, the dentist and cocaine.
Sam Cooke songs make the city okay.

Stolen Twizzlers are just gross edible red sticks
 of nothing,
like steam punks of nothing's worth with ironic
mustaches.

Killallyourdarlings.
You disappear so well...so can I.

This song brings me back, in mind memory,
to little stairs on Conselya Street,
and a laundry mat on Meeker Avenue,
propoganda for every man like me.

I am apologetically saturated,
today is not Friday.

Which way is the Middle, which way is the Midwest?
Up.

White Harlem World

I sit on the stoop
and wait for my nigga, Daniel
to finish work.

I write rhyming poetry,
for once,
and watch the world.

The cars are going crazy.
Every Honda wants to get home
to their families
Because of the rain.

I believe
in between the beers
that I am getting better at life,
but I still wake up every morning
with all these new fears,
and the only thing I trust is the ghetto,
because the ghetto is never to be trusted.

And in that...
the ghetto smiles by borrachos and glocks,
and we are red-bearded whiteboys buying it all
with books and bags of weed.
We are gentrification.
Wastes of nothing.

The smell of Puerto Rican food
stops my writing.

I look up and see cops beating some kid.
I think Vernon or Daniel may know
that blind, bloody thug
who is, at this moment in time,
getting his ass handed to him by batons.

Elaine Vick

Her bones are made of watermelon seeds,
so says her wayward son, my best friend.

Daycare teacher,
likes to party away
the weekends
at The Corkroom on Goldenrod Road;
I once saw her drink gasoline mixed with milk.

She puked up hot Sprite.

A Southerner,
who loves her kids to death,
grew up in an orange grove,
has twenty-six tattoos, all dolphins

She owns a mobile home in each of the fifty states.

In Florida, she has a boat on top
of a boat on top of her mobile home.

I am not trying to write bullshit here.
She lives a certain dream.
Her son and I are jealous.
Mostly of the vision of the Vick.

She still calls French fries *Freedom Fries*.
She was a professional jet-skier for two weeks,
but she gave that up to be a daycare teacher.
Her pork chops are delicious,

and
she slaughters the hogs herself;
she shoots them point blank with a revolver.

One time, at the zoo,
she put a Marlboro cigarette out on a lion cub.
She is really good at rollerblading.
She is gonna kick my ass after reading this shit.
She created a time machine out of Kleenex
and then destroyed it, blew it away.

She always made me take my vitamins.

Poem

I was with my buddy,
Brown Brother Dave,
 last evening,
all.

We got drunk.
We got high.
We played some music.
We did our best to forget.

I know David through Puppy Jones.
He moved west to east, despondent
about a year ago.

Last night he was
upset about a girl
he has been fingering
for a month.

Last week, I told him not to fall in love.
This week he did.
Last week I was in love.
This week I am not.

Archipelago

See what I mean, Sea?
I told you, I am not an island.
Hear the series.
clear the mirrors.
Statue, scared stiff,
send me hand-written letters.
over clouds behave.
get grey, good girl.
cheers to movies without sequels.

Foes, Sweet Fire

Lack of imagination,
foes, watermelon sugar, fire...
doesn't mean I am a writer:
I am just an archeologist.

I spill
the rest of me as a mastermind,
a paradisiacal itinerant poet,
with only a tomahawk and some Belief.

Won't you still be my country song?
Old school.
Trains
and Rivers.

It is raining
and the opposite sex
is mad at me,
but I have a falcon.

The Overheards
of the Grilled Cheese Night

The night was thin on any kind of love,
thick on wind due to approaching winter.
The windows rattled.

I let the hammerhead
collide with the nail,
hanging up a framed photo
in my new bedroom.

I heard a voice coming from the airshaft
on the 89th street side of the building.
The voice was on the phone
for I only heard responses and repeating reprieves.

I made myself a grilled cheese sandwich
and watched basketball on tv.
I heard my neighbor knocking
on something next-door.
I heard her crying, too.
I heard her say to herself,
"I'm sorry, but I am not cut out for this anymore."

Witness Brad's Elbow

Mouth and shins wide open:
drink fast, love fast;
the time to hesitate is through.

The funny bone of Bradley
is numb yet assisting his hand
with another shot of whiskey.

Watch him go.
Watch him die.
With a scholarship in his eye.

Bloodshed Software

After the last poem,
what do you expect?

Our hero never turns around.
He hides at Tin Lizzies in New York City
and pretends to like football.

He never gets nervous anymore.

Small fox photographs,
he likes to dream.
Cocaine before noon,
then the dentist.

Borne.
He is real.
Or soon
will be real.
He is a window.
Forget him
for now.

He will find the chain-link fence and climb it
and cut the shit outta his right wrist on the barbwire
and he doesn't have health insurance.

The next day,
I am waiting for the day,
I know I have the heart,

I am hoping that I die today,
But love beats every time.

I am him
with slit wrists.
I told you this story
ends in bloodshed.

He is me
w/ everything.
every thing.

Since I Saw You
on the Last Saturday
of Life

postcards are funny in this day and age.
sending one is almost a novelty these days.
I cut my hair and trimmed my beard.
only trimmed, though; I may have a beard forever.
it's the second best decision I ever made.
you know the first, dear.
you missed a good panhandler fight in the Pearl,
punk rock kids arguing over beat-up guitars.
lasted an hour.
Holliday left again, said he'll be back in a year.
ran into Shy-Shy at Prost!
I broke my pinky knuckle a few weeks ago.
don't ask.
started working at a bookstore.
published a few short stories in Canada.
the best beer and the best lunatics, here.
Oh, shit that reminds me!
I saw both Kelly's.
He says hi, she says hi.
They aren't together, by the way. Thank god.
I am still going to Montreal soon.
Maybe October.
maybe meet my Someone.
will visit Michel's grave, doubtless.
the dark leaves theme keeps playing.
hope you are well.
don't ever give up.

(undress me)

everyone asks me to write them a fucking poem...

hatchet doing, undress me.

foolish and still smiling,
with wine under rain clouds,
trying for shots in the dark,
while smoking in shadows
and trying to restore an old fighting light.

sideways action on sidewalks.
destruction in birthday cards.

this is all fairly true,
but not falsely fair.
this love song ends and another begins;
did you ever think the earth would quake for me once
more?

at least scream, blue, a town with a little more in me.
while I bleed and forget why I am bleeding.
a layer of dust that I can't bring myself to clean.
because this dust was here before I got here.

this is this,
and I can't carry poems.
thank you for the beautiful betrayal.

...and I'm sorry for kicking that dog.

Banners and Last Minute Blueprints

rat rent miscommunication comes
every month
for all of us.
like periods and problems.
love doesn't come that often, ask bastard Hashem.
we all forget to sleep.
you are as good as you reciprocate.
marquis diamonds are mine.
they sit in a filing cabinet.
with curses and old anger.
surprises aren't worth the burning paper.
I stab coins in a cylinder.
and forgiveness without pictures.
growing secret roses in the thistle, ray ray.
in the bristly bushes behind the house.
I don't need kismet to give it time.
call me after you get off the citybus.
help my find my cunning.
this could be the most precious moment of your life.
the tendency is to push it as far as you can.
as sick as sick gets.
hold me up.
like a banner.
build me up.
like a blueprint building.
look at me like the future looks at the past.

A Small, Shaky Poem

I come in pieces.

we only have one goodbye to get right.

let's listen to old folk songs.
and take the train to some long land.
I believe it is surrounded by water.
but then again, so are we.
I know you're not stupid.
you can do long division.
I miss your face on my face.
but I don't miss you.
there's work to do.
growing old is something new.
I am a blacksmith, not a surgeon.
my hands shake near your hands.
because they haven't seen each other's palms
in so long.
Candles and hamburgers and romance.
There's grace, but it is not mine.
Take me back to Asheville or Nashville in the snow.

By the Prefident

A grover, a watcher, a teller,
signed by thousand,
even though today I wear ugly orange
and walk between sky and water
with red wrists and a talking sewn giraffe,
my only pal out west.
needless to say, she stands
out
out,
out.

Adios, I say.
to the day and the way,
to the tribute and the rifle beach,
to the spots,
to the vaulted ceilings.

A leftover layover,
hours of doubt and boredom
in the middle
of America as
I guess at silver,
and wish for lakes again.

promises are exploding via email,
bullets in bourbon,
airports and trainstations
are the only honest places,
even in lies and letdowns,

to feel me.

Watching movies in my mind
of past lives,
signed off long ago.
I guess giving up is all that is left,
but I will procrastinate as usual.
God knows, I am good at that.

Forward she sells,
yelling like steam.
I see the streets and the ants,
the hills and hammocks.
the ships in the sound,
the regrets, boundless, enjoyable.

this is the way I believe in.

take my hand.
take my sentence.

animals were

the mammals stuck in my teeth.
    were bones before hearts.

invertebrates,
I can't have you.
I can't help you.

on fire on the moon.
inside inspiration arriving in the dark.

fuck umbrellas.
and fuck luck.
      I still want a little more.
I am not sure what this has to do with last night.
but I brave.
and steal this all away from everyone else.

live alive.
like your new days, dear.
animals were us.
good terms.
all acoustic hearts, beating, significant.

**don't let what was
 get in the way of what's next**

sweeping.
back and forth.
broom and bucket.
relaxed and wondering why.

listening to *I Remember* by Devendra.
better than Bon Iver tonight,
because it is all meaningless.
I guess at hospitals.

start at the front
of the restaurant.
swing the glass into a pile,
turn to the magnificent mop.

the corners of my mouth
are turned upward into a thing
called a smile,
and I don't even realize it
until the song ends.

leave the faucet on.
turn off the fan by the bar.
swipe at leftover bullets.
endlessly, I won't change.

sweeping.
back and forth, hursting crows, too.

to Somewhere.
relaxed and wondering where.

Poor Poem

there's something beautiful about being poor.
and I am poor as shit.

get some other diamonds sparkling.
loser am I, en route.

and you are absolutely stunning.

pens are my scratching fortune.
but I write only to spontaneously combust.

time to do the dishes and think about tomorrow.

four five zero three nine

it is four thirty in the eastern sky.
excuse me.

the day has let clouds get the better of me.
I am a little late for life.
an asshole at best.

the earth spins beneath me.
the world turns in my chest.
and I am left with leftovers.
free from memory, injured soul.

this bottle of wine.
spends the night inside my garage.
oh how I have missed the Rumbler.
and I never thought I would.

ignorance is a lake.
love is a river.

the nurses and the criminals will come.
I hope my phone vibrates for me.
an accident, possibly.

news came of a wild horizon.
in your good.
new environment.
fine gone.
I open an umbrella on the airplane.
just in spite of badluck.

let's talk about yaks.
and the past.
over Magic Hat #9.

I can't wait to find level ground.

Here, Already

I kick wolf,
light lighter,
spend silver certificate,
good, better, get a blood blister,
here already.

I time travel,
stab summer,
wear bracelets,
lose coasters,
here already.

I knuckle cracks,
save,
money mischief,
cobble,
here already.

I cancel nights,
continue days,
frank four afternoons,
generate thirds,
here already.

I kill condors,
catch ketchup,
fight hands,
forget friends,
here already.

118

I wish over drawbridges,
wish for her,
connect the dots,
fight for feathers on backs,
here already.

I dance,
and sing,
and live,
and love,
here already.

take the train and fuck off

we are hall of famers,
traveling from sure to shore,
begging for forgiveness,
and finding it hard to maintain a sense of quorum
and contractual dignity.

fines will come with crimson ex crimes,
the ones against our creative souls.
any art is good for us.
leave me alone, I guess.

the stink of the land,
past tense,
might whisper
this way north and give up on me forever,
but I don't dig musical graves
or bullshit symphonies of the future;
I enjoy the regrettable now.

task force hands,
chewing jumper-cable lips,
door-knobs eye sockets,
these pointless possibilities are like old shoes,
and old ships,
and old loves,
unforgettable thank-you's.

so thank you.
for reading this bullshit,
and eating biscuits in the west,

and commenting on my stupid eyes,
with stupid eyes, yourselves,
always stupid eyes on traveling trains,
with the bouncing tunes of pork and hammers,
and lazy love.

manyseptembersanddecembers

the holes in this city
are cheese mysteries
since you left the existential earth,
and
I swirl my glass just to stay bored.

crushed water,
she sings to me,
you are she,
and there is no way out of this sitting fire.

all the birds
beyond that sheet window
are heading for southern Decembers,
and we are heading to the future.

happy as can be in this sea
of weird smells and lost trains
and cold Junes,
like we were supposed to wait for this year.

please darling,
sing with me forever
and we will count Decembers,
forever.

I like repeating curtain words,
summer sucks,
your Christmas parts can comfort me,
indeed.

stash your love next to me
with pheasants and peasants
and barbed wire walls,
that we will break down, inevitably.

whoa there is wear
in the upcoming September
and
I haven't forgotten peaches or bracelets
or nights in the roaring wind.

we walk by our nights,
your father is singing in leaves,
about the complications of love and life,
and I am just trying to be a *we*.

We Will

the clouds had chosen to banish the sun.
before black flock fog.
the type that moves down orange stairwells.
forgiving the night of its healthy fear.
patience in stars on shoulders.
the wilderness, too, is benevolent.

with new perfect pride.
old rivers and new soap and new gold.
I join the pier with pop postage.
railroads and pure kisses.

I say this with famous fangs:
We Will find something in tomorrow, today.

I Am Roosevelt

an elbow to the face does not feel good.
it kind of feels like an elbow to the face.
nonetheless, it is not Friday anymore.
and I am bleeding.
badly.

I lost a lot of shoes in the war.
growing old is something new.
I wish I had the guts to be good.

the storm rolls up the East River.
and turns east towards Greenpoint.
fuck Portland.
for now.
torn apart by existence and existing.
and trying to explain to myself that this is it.
with soap in my eyes, a loose tooth,
and a crackling heart that is trying not to burn.

I don't need a new life,
just a better place to die.

This is Big

I like the mornings.
Unlike everyone.
I like Mondays.
Let's go canoeing.
in the shower.
Let's tie a banner.
around the neck of forever.
I like the mornings.
I love to listen.
isn't there a warning?
or something to drink?
just mention it all.
life is for little things.
but this is big.
as a bus.
eyes and bullshit.
it's all worth it.
listen to the city sing.
with me.
angry orchard and whiskey.
there are a lot of Trevors.
in this world.
and seagulls.
and sluts.
ever forget if you locked your door?

Poem

I am you.

it feels like tomorrow but it is today

I am serious Saturday.
but it is casual Friday.
Flip-flops never.
for Heaven's sake.
I am drunk.
what did you do today?
it is not raining.
day off blues.
sorry state.
it is finally time to laugh.
and find something to say.
is it catsup or ketchup?
darling, misery.

Peninsula

    come on, pretty lady,
talk to me.
we are meant to be.

    hey! that rhymed!

I have a few plans for your birthday.
Bon Iver and never losing again and peach pie and
water on three sides.

and saxophone and piano.
and me.

    be my girl and I will be your world.

I crack my knuckles honestly.
and break my side ribs just to make you think about
laughter.

this will warm.

expect us.

Condor

I slowed down after work.
and hit the stoop with Kayle and Shy Shy.
she turned off her phone to ignore me.
and Vernon has drugs but Vernon is nowhere to be
found.

Kayle shows first with rats and booze
and cigarettes.
Shy Shy shows second with mosquitoes
and pizza.

Hey Booger! I yell.
we all worked long shifts.
we make noise on the street.
I text her again. Nada.

  dear Reader,
I hope your heart hurts.
metaphors scurry too.
we spend too much money.
white wine hills with bicycle locks,
the three of us aren't out for blood.
just forgotten minutes, friends.
as rivers bleed right by us.

these are my feet, made of sentences.
I stand tall.
a fool.
in the cigarette night.

I hold the door for an old woman.
and a chef.

who knows for sure.
I dream of my Montreal hair.
a dump truck drives by.

I am locked in an elevator.
and still pressing up.

perfect free dumb

a generous amount of bourbon.
equal parts sweet vermouth.
and dry vermouth.
a dash or two of bitters.
served up.
with music and city.
no Carl, Daniel?
I am uptown, too.
in a land of neighborhoods.
silly liars like me.
black bear poachers with red front doors.
always open.
we will change.
doubtless.
I hold my heart with my hands.
I hold my hands with yours.

hotel species

eight minutes blue.
so glass slow dance.
we harvest the day for its hours.
the song laughs on in lonely hawk.
fashion pretending at gunpoint.
shoot for six.
party long.
windows will break by my bones.
same shirt since miniature lions.
this is the day the river dies.

ok which

my legs might make it there
with the rest of my body
dragged along as
brains and luggage.

I am happy
to meet you in the middle.
maybe at Dottie's True Blue Cafe.
in San Francisco!

it is not Tuesday.
it is a special occasion.
it is something sweetly revived.
it's been long enough.

drink with me after ten.
kill this Concrete Noun with me.
tell me about letters.
my sternum creaks like an old house.

sauce, secret, witch,
picture how life could've been.
embarrassingly,
every little thing...is possible.

Two Bluejays in D Major

pissing in the East River.
like old times.
I wish it were raining.
we are pressured by the summer to be outside.
a marathon of minutes.
and I don't associate with people with morals.

I toss a microwave and a phone into the shallow water.
youth was the place, the shore.

welcome.
an epic setting.
surfeit.
a day with a day.
twelve finish lines.
and indeed, I will let you pick the lunette time.
as of stone or wood.

a point-of-view, over there.
a lady and a tiger.
a painting of the trees that are outside.
my aperture.
and it's birds.
and those birds' friends.

I could dream tonight.
I could scream.
but I just smile.
spider webs catch nightmares.
I will share it with you, dear.

later on this fine wine afternoon.
right when the sun decides to die.
when it is time to retire.

the striped fire outside will stay.

Muddy

leavin' soon.
as long as your heart is underwater
or you are sleeping through this.

"the Sun is me."

it's better to be compared to garbage cans
than to nothing.

poetry is life distilled.
I raise my glass.
here's to honor.

"there's a fly on your hat."

things got good.
you made me write.
Meet me in Montreal in October.

Dinner and Sometimes Everything

as the sun burns down,
I have trifling nickel dinners
with dime dead persons.

I halo the whores
and fight a war
through dinosaur hair
and bastard hopes.

of fire,
I am real,
we are real,
and we dance the dance of distant life;
it's a banal crap-shoot
with heartburn and popular puppets,
on our own, always:
always love,
always evenings,
always yours.

cheeseburgers and television,
puppies and babies
are background sounds
and midtown sights
for champions.

share
cocktails under the billiards table
that isn't really there
and we

disappear, here.
as I get too inebriated,
too haunted,
I eat my words.

hope is a currency, I agree, Tommy the Poet,
in our universe,
pass the salt.
here, skies are clear of nicks
and my friends are better than me.
I am a shoplifter
with some sort of motion inside,
wild.

I love you, Serenade,
I really do,
and the table is set on the ninth hole
of a golf course
in a living room
without a trendy *shroof*
and neither of us can find
the light switch.

Indolent

I lay in hotel bed.
shirt on the floor, not on me.
I'm eating banana pancakes.
Hello! to the silly sun.
my phone is dead.
my right eye twitches an open omen.
They never close again.
never flood.
newness and air.
There's whiskey in the coffee.
The coffee sits between my knees.
no work, Monday.
I can hear the ocean.

Burn the Moon

Burn the moon, too, night.
Shampoo the stars.
Look up.
And make the sky simply grin.
Tomorrow.
Cut that tooth off my toe.
Dead epic with the scissors.
You made me live write.

Pieces of a Poem

maybe it is bricks and mortar now.
out me in your marrow.

no one has ever been kissed like this.

since.

just a little tired from a funeral.
working later tonight.
hope to choke to death.
join friend in that silly last bed.

not drunk.
wish I were drunk.
I don't like these people.

there is still the matter of the dog.

I miss Dylan.

I clap as loud as I can.
find an empty street.

I have necks on my neck.

I bet you'll get a lot of compliments down in hell.

I don't need fate to give it time.

I walk around in old jeans

with a busted zipper.

it's funny.

this is a poem for people with broken hearts.

warm Rolling Rocks in this before-noon life.
I wanted to be tall.

a hair-cut to the head.
the sound of these typer keys.
we all forget to sleep.
we all pretend to keep.
I don't have to exist.

outside.
this.
place.

I just have to live.
in you.
you look so beautiful.

I write a letter on an old dollar bill,
thanking the skyrockets for forever.

I tack the dollar on the wall.
and make a phone call to the girl of my dreams.
thanking her for sticking around.

even though my fingers are dirty.
even though I am sweaty.

even though I pee in the shower.

I am forever.
I am not places.
I am here.

Arrows

Nothing happens
and
it keeps not happening,
Forever

WALLETS

I.

Three years. Three years. Three years!

You are as far from Tallahassee as I am.
You are as far from Atchison, Kansas as I am.
You are about as far from that Brooklyn apartment,
with free dust and guitars,
as I am.

Seems so close, yet so far.

The population of a needy muted television.
Your hair is in my beard,
and a two-ton hour glass.

II.

I can't change histories.

I once blanketed Hollywood.
I told girls lies,
like the month was June
when it was really July.
They would have found out anyway
at the bank.

"She wouldn't make it out West," he said.
I told him to "fuck off!"

After all, he wasn't royalty.
He scrubbed restaurants
for wallets,
and got skinny on yak,
and cigarettes.

Though,
she, a cruel world
to the young girl she was once.
Enjoy June, ignorantly.
September will come
and will treat you differently.

Goddamn these airplanes.

III.

Sick with broken ribs.
Three years is three years.

Silver children say
God died in his sleep,
so I invented raccoon skeletons.
We can't stay here tonight.
The waitress hates us,
and the black phrase coyote
is the origin of death.

In the morning
we will hit the river,
and eat bananas and poetry,
and drift along in strife,

in life,
drinking orange Gatorades
by the bedside.

I wrap my books in tin foil.
I send thank-you cards to the month of August
for the clarity, finally,
and the dead friends still living.

Life is like ladders that lead nowhere;
everybody wants something to "do" tonight.

I just German lunched, then cocained
and basketballed;
all good for the heart.
I shout about love in silence.
I sneeze.
I curse cold vodka afternoons.
I science poetry with verbs.

Hope is a currency,
like my friend Tom says on stage.
Then the heart-attack guitar starts,
and I hear Brooklyn screams.

IV.

There is a mirror in a hallway,
the hallway is not mine.
I jump rope and knock the pictures from the walls
out of accidental spite.

148

There is such a thing,
and violence is in my whispered past,
but patience is currently resting on my simple
shoulders.

I use an old ladder to change a light bulb,
video grass through the kitchen window
with chicken wire for squirrels;
this is some sort of fucked-up long division,
eight divided by eight divided by eight divided by
eight.

See?

Q: What Do You Call Someone Who Plays the Bugle?
A: a Bugler

this is the sad sack of margarette devil business, shit!
lettuce get a party going.
but you gotta check the expiration date.

you're a little fucker, important.
but you are the only one who knows what time it is.
no one else has a watch.

italicize the name of sirens.
the ones on horizons.
and I will forgive your forever.

goddamn it.

splayed

it's not the day for squab pies.
lemonwater, yes. inspiration, maybe.
punk rock, shitpits, twisted, red details, definitely.
stealing poetry from bookstores.
with my goddamn name on the cover.
yesterday's black BMW was a funlunch.
she has adult legs, more freedom above.
kaleidoscope thoughts.
both whiskey and scotch.
and turkey sandwiches.
two-forty five, keep maladies alive.
my mustache is sticky.
there are a lot of junkies in this part of the city.
there are murals of miniature lions.
there are eyes that are happy.
there are huge events of incompetence.
there are tulips in the middle of the table.
look at that pretty orange thing running across the
street.
a dress, a dog, all of it and us in the middle of it all.
she licks the stout molasses out of my mustache.
and we call it a day.

Honest Breakfast

exit tune
going above heads,
'cause they listen
but they can't hear.
only we can hear this song.
there's a butt
at the window
smoking his thirteenth
"last" cigarette.
there's idiots daring fun in the front row.
they are deaf to this.
while the rhythm section
stands through brass
and the orrery breathes
through the most beautiful eyes,
I hope the rain don't come too soon.
never been crazy like this.
the stairs task the bag,
dance with honest, small neighborhoods.
men make decisions,
and decisions make men.
I sing and I settle into this,
and I scream my fucking arms off
from this cinnamon mountain.
We replicate the fix live,
co-producers of our own solar system.
keys are keys,
fashion the world an Audience
to our wonderful show.

King Love Thing

I keep you regal
on a ring on my pinky
as I collect candy
the color of tin cans.

I worship the tall grass
where the coyotes live
as you say,
soon, we will be ghosts, too.

I worship you
taken by a better day
when there were no
believable bones in our broken hearts.

I sit upright on my thrown,
try better posture,
while I just want to hold you
and tell you that you are the most beautiful thing in
the wide wide world.

I've been walking around
this town for so long;
I got some money
but no soul.

I've been trying
to have a habit,
and waiting for the leaves
of the tree to turn upside down for rain.

I walk through Brooklyn
Monday mornings
and I look for a timemachine,
I look for you.

I've been radioactive
for a few weak weeks now
the days without the fresh, the road,
the days without you.

Driving Around Queens
in a "Borrowed" Car
(with all the windows rolled down)

baby, you were the wind,
and I can't wait to begin
blinking again.

the yellow scarves of the world
set the middle ground scenes
for a person like me,
with fathoms-deep emotions,
obviously.

this rain is a gift.
the windows stay down.
my face gets wet.
this adventure is the not end (of dreaming).
this place is a heart defect.
this life is mine,
and sometimes it's fun as hell.

tempestuous hope
is a friend of God's.
this is some sort of folk song.
it's easier to quit.
my teeth are cold
so I knock on them for good luck.

goodnight, boulevards, let's begin anew.
on a stolen Tuesday in the rain.

the six songs of brick red

we used crayons.
on the concrete porch.
then I left around noon.
I forgot my favorite hat at your apartment.
it's probably still on your dresser.

I walked towards Ladd's Addition.
SE 34th street.
you know that hill?
with the bricks.

at the top of said lonely hill,
I saw a different pretty girl
walking down the descent.
she was wearing a white sundress and an overcoat,
just in case of always rain...
and she had this nice big smile stretching
across her world.
she was dumbly gazing forward and up,
and just smiling the most genuine smile
in all the world.
I wondered what created that smile.
she danced by and disappeared,
and subsequently, without ever knowing it,
she made my day a little bit better.

the lion blood papers, part 2

always wanted to be a lion,
maybe because the name.
I am nothing but a scout coyote,
hence the name of this shit.

whenever I try to do great
by the sighing luminance
of the wayward world,
I just make the thing bloody worse.

anti-apex, keystone, Lascaux, and literature,
yet confrontations kill us down
to failed Fridays and forgotten dakotas,
leaving the jackal a pawn to die with borrowed laugh
sides.

(*I'd settle for being a snow leopard or a giraffe, or, better yet,*
  a red-tailed hawk, or one of the owls)

There will never be a part one.

Kill Me Off This Street

I am still a child,
but it doesn't matter,
I shake so violently
with the best idiots.

jobless and honest,
my mom was right,
you can't fucking win
in this world.

been battling life.
live the dash, man.
whisper to rattle snakes
and dream of trains.

Abigail, that one sentence made my fucking day.

Lies are more lovely.
I'm gonna go get a haircut.

where poets go

breakfast in bodegas.
libertine lunch.
dinner on ships.
57th street, between 10th and 11th.
dive bars.
the bank.
the post office.
bookstores to steal books.
reggae show in Brooklyn.

anywhere.

hell.

all the rage

when colors become this beautiful
and people seemingly, maybe even truly, are good,
patience is the icing on the cake.

sponsored by Hot Pockets and pickles,
provided by sunny days, unemployment, and love.
inspired by true life events.

this is a hit film.

what made today so great?

good news.
good girl.
good soup.
bad coffee.
rain.
good music.
great dialogue.

no line at the post office.
no chapped lips.

good pizza.
good south.
good Canadian whiskey.
my basketball team lost.
but it's okay

I didn't have to work today.

thank you so much

my hands are red wine,
and while I still don't know what love means,
I picture you holding a picture of me.

I'm in a cab,
meet me in the past.
your skirt says it all,
and the shape of your body
says you love forever me.

don't second guess your fear,
you were right from the start:
love is loud!
venom is venom.
I'd rather be bold than brave.

162

Between Lexington and Park

we can find great mornings, this.
volatile but greatest, the.

save this spring day on stamps.
put the stamps on post
and mail it to myself.

stoned eyes, wooden glasses, purple glasses,
some sort of delicious kismet.
it's hard to remember the end of December.

there was some sort of meteor shower,
and I thanked the goddamn daytime sky for telling me
why.

we live for warm mornings like this.

This One

there are certain poems
that I don't want to give to anyone.
a few make me want to be selfish.
put them in a box or a drawer,
and read them over sandwiches
on my midnights.

Yourself, Rose

there I was just galloping along,
and eating chicken and drinking gin.

hi. how are you?
I'm fine, she said dead.

there's a rose in the center of town.

where the streets meet,
the eclipse of lovely misses
tears down pre-war buildings.

I don't know what that looks like anymore.

songbird, be seen.
you showed up and changed everything.

Desmond Sidewalk

Meeker Street.
regret.
last summer.
last line.
gold fun.
the roof.

I descend her stairs to soundtracks.

These are songs.
given to someone else.
bloody hands.
mine.

be better.

recreate us.

we can do no harm.
After our harm.

this will be a better year.
I promise.
but, sick quip,
we only have four hands.

Everything

exist.

hear in color.

sweet woods, the night.

dark the light.
light the dark with your ukulele.

elbow operatic, indeed,
I dare you to be more beautiful
than you already are
to me.

Poem.

the earth is one big loud place

I'm writing this in silence.
but there is no such thing.
my neck hurts loud.
love is loud.
trucks are loud.

the earth is one big loud place.

full of snakes and rakes and
the iniquitous day dreams of man.

my heart is loud.

this poem should be read very loud.

useful things

poets are dreamers.
novelists are liars.

I am both.

real men don't apologize.

I guess I am not
a real man.

you can't laugh when you are dead.

I am not useful
anymore.

I don't understand how the world works.

I just know that you can't win in it.

the bones in my heart
are melting.

four inches from dying.
rain and rope.

I am a reservoir poet.
I am an insomniac as of late.

the songlines of the half king,

me,
a stray animal,
are narrow and strange,
and as short as life is long.
unrepairable.

vanish.

Tennessee

what do all these songs have in common?
she says these wayward breaths from underneath a
useless umbrella.
there are a million tiny things, moments, that make
happiness possible.
we don't talk about our pasts.

I whisper lyrics into the most
beautiful left and right.
we go south but higher,
where two rivers meet in Wednesday's woe.
my hands hold the neck of the woods nearby.

she was a damn good kisser.
I am still after last night.
it's all part of the adventure.
stand still in it with me.

Consider Us the Rulers of the Universe

scotch blue afternoons with buildings,
I found a nickel heads-up.

his only and his
have
spread these days.

better nights are beside me...

this isn't the first time
I've been a complete asshole,
nor will it be the last.

blood in the street, blood in the yard.

belly up to a barstool,
that's how we live,
we wake up with bad conduct.

forget me not, forever,
always whispering fun,
or surprise in winter;
your cornerstone still hits the spot.

we talk on and on in internet eyes,
and shake.
We try for the dead.

she crosses her broken heart...

forgive me in a hurry.
in every book I ever read
there is a line that sticks out to me.

lock my keys inside my
home tonight,
better wolves be asking
for heart and driftwood
and horizon.

Salt Milk

appeal to hammers,
we will gallop west
for soup and paychecks,
only returning in two Junes
to where the trains exit the earth.

even if her words
broke some palace,
and we all put it back together
again...
you will still see the cracks.

an inexplicable act of self destruction
dressed in fine satin and lace,
the world to me,
and each bluest blue is mine,
hidden among the mornings that mourn.

jones love question marks within wet weather,
from the first time our eyes shook hands,
we were more than just moments;
listen to a certain song
and do not give it to anyone else.

The ATM

It's always 20.
Fast cash.
No receipt.
For I don't want to be reminded
of how poor I am.

It's sometimes deposits.
during business hours.
Mainly Fridays.
Payday.

I always look at the leftover receipts.
Dropped by careless rich people prior.
Always with available balances far greater than mine.

I wrote this poem.
While on a cash/lemon/booze run.
On someone else's rich receipt.

Eat Some Crow

The sweetheart returns
to voodoo rivers
with a new down,
a chance at some sort of weird redemption.

What are you doing this weekend?
She said.
Becoming Thunder.
I said.

Then the heat drunk comes
with escaping life
and I am canoeing away,
so please look after my sisters.

You don't know
how it feels to be alive
until you know how it feels
to die.

Concertina Wire

Scene One

there was a fire at the B&B,
right next to the news agent,
on the same block as stranger-lovin' Dan.

werd on the street is no one got seriously injured.
that makes me glad,
but now where are we going to buy our
3am stoop 40s?

Scene Two

meet me at the TGIFridays in Penn Station.
soon.
I am off of work from both jobs
for a while,
long story.

Scene Three

sorry,
not going to meet you in BK tonight.

Scene Four

starts with the slamming of a door.
I eat rose petals, get going
and fuck it all.
my rib cage rips.

the laundry ain't put away.
seven months into this year,
it still feels like last year.

on view through August

I work in music and movies,
not in mistaken words,
not anymore,
misspelled in burning literature.
Always.

the sounds of chains.
somewhere a name.
and fissures.
from broken rocks.
and bank accounts.

I am headed for the land.
of snow and socks.
and fireside tipples.
turn off the kitchen light.
turn off the living room.

you will see a girl.
in a galley south.
a cross between Kansas and the Island.
silly with it.

I am just a stranger on some uncertain shore.
and honestly, I just spilled beer on myself.
telling tales out of school.
stupid.
stinks in that old barb.
a sack of hay and hey in Travers Hollow.

I Got Stabbed Today

as it were,
I always get stabbed to death on a Monday.

this time round,
'twas over the phone
with lovely laughter
and secret alliteration.

it started in the arm,
and ended up
dancing in the kitchen heart.

wounded with wonder and waiting,
like before,
but with helpful bleedings,
surely breathing, wearing haunted windchimes,
a poet I am not.

The Spooky Forest

Like the duplication
of a duplication
of a haunted airplane,
love still exists underwater.

She says my name as she hangs up the phone,
"Goodnight, Ryan Marcel."

Poem

just one more day to dream.

sometimes hate is as close as you can get
to love.

I have to make dinner and war first.

your hands are capable
of making beauty and righteousness.
left is for decor, right is for justice.

we go from the Upper East to the Lower East.

the taxicabs drive through the street.

I am a servant of some sort of destiny.

I simply scribble trees and meadows
and
you and me.

Re: Montreal

I didn't know
then
the weight of my tongue
or the story
behind the artist.

Through every shadow
of a darker shade of blue,
there was you.

the dead will rise,
boisterous and full of turpitude.

Demon claws,
and you taking a picture
of me
as I fall down the stairs!

You Must Make These Werds
Your Home

just pretend everything is okay...

Don't break life in half.
Werds were few.
Written in dark eyes.
Just kids in the backyard drinking wine.
I've walked with you through the woods.
I've wondered with you in rooms.

don't remember to tell me to forget.

Doors: 8pm
Show: 9pm

this is my sheep date.

And
sixteen eyes in the living room.
optometrists, pretty sure.
Listen to Minor Threat records.

I saw a ghost at 11:48pm.
a terrible friend in the attic.
can't hide in covers.
can't cut holes in the linens.

Cheers!
here's to pine trees and everything being good again.

Snails and Nails

Do you know what a crocodile is?

Playing Nails
while
Myles from The Drums
says he can't, nay, he won't come to this side of town,
as
guns sound off
somewhere nearby.

Nails is a game
of throwing hammers in the air
while holding
a big beer.

I throw garden snails
at Franco.

My shoes are good at chewing.
The mosquitoes in this Brooklyn backyard
are multicolored and numerous.

The sun sets.
Shy Shy shows up with more booze.
I hear the ice cream man,
and smell weed.

Bleeding out of my hand
from hammer throwing.

In 2001,
I was 18...
Or sad.
What time is it? Monday?
Or August?

Night Surfing on Opium

The black blanket sea,
engulfing me and eating my legs.
I am a pawn or a fawn,
dancing with brown eyes.
I don't need sleep,
I have dreams.
I feel for the swells.
I never want to leave this black space place.
Problems don't follow you
out onto the Atlantic Ocean.
I believe these are the same stars
that I saw in Brooklyn
during that sweet, sad, sweaty summer.

Also, I was fifteen fifteen years ago.

Racecar Spelled Backwards is Racecar

ricochet.
this way.

make dinner.
and sweet memories.
get lost.
with nothing.
but adventure.

whatever we are passionate about.
exist in it.
like a falcon.

there are people on bicycles.
wearing hope.
as a noose.

there are people in haunted airplanes.
waiting.

repair to living.

Young God

Label us young gods
with the length of long hands,
singing
like California
while
pleasing your past,
a little vine
wrapped around
time.

Let's have a glass of wine,
Franco,
and let's have another glass of wine.

Only a hobo,
but one more.

No more than that.
No more than this
night.

by six

as
sweetly as the day's minutes and moments
tick sickly away
into the things we call
the past,
I march towards tomorrow
with a different violin spin.

odd
goodnight, living room,
the one with the flowers
left behind
by the blind backs
of hatchets and pineapples.

look
at that blue petrichor
of yesterland's hillside romance,
tap your prefix,
a fine gone fire
burning slow and low.

live
like company free,
please,
don't destroy me.

Shake with Me

This is a song
for anyone who is
happy and sad
at the same time...

down the hall,
passed the bedroom,
the kitchen waits
with open cabinet eyes
for this to die.

Cook it up, she says,
burn it and discard it and drink it,
I don't care.

The fridge leaves the building,
dancing until time slows,
and eventually stops,
and I am altogether falling apart.

I shake,
just as the horizon eats the ocean,
as sure as the stars are nicks
in the glass sky,
justice shy shies,
and I shake violent
qith the best lunatics
in the business.

I was standing,

still bleeding,
still asking for a tap dance.

A Burrowed Muse

I heard you've been dancing
in another kitchen
with chicken pickles and manicotti karate
and goddamn olives and god and pizza bagels
and that lighthouse,
the one with the peeling paint,
Ours.

Free Question Marks For Sale

Nearer
to Hashem
up here
where the leaves fly
and drop seeds
that grow birds.

This is my first poem
written while sitting in the sky.

I ate a burger
with bacon and blue cheese,
because life is short.

My Heart is Bigger Than the Hearth

this shoreline day,
known as now, today,
the sea laps at the sand,
seemingly so far away,
as I go to the ATM
in a city so close, yet so far from the sea.

I fastcash twenty dollars
and head to Brooklyn.
I am not looking forward to any of this.

I'll be working
in Willytowne tonight,
on Bedford and Metropolitan.

I don't think I ever loved you,
but the world is dying to meet you.

Do you know how many times
I have been told
that I am a bad friend?

six.

Some love was made for the lights,
or making noise.

Iocan't see the stereo
Or the vacuum.

Life spins slower
than the rotation
of the Earth,
and my legs are tired
from running and jumping.

Act like you've been here before.
Brick.

She sings
while smiling
and it's hard to figure out things.

I'm trying
to understand
something some refer to
as life, lately.

What are you doing?
she said.
I'm building.
I replied.

I live to love you.
I am a love letter away.
I am not eager,
your eyes.

I was in a truck
that drove your street
last night,
I held my breath,

and looked up
at your windows,
no lights were on,
and I
am still under you.

Let The Violins Kick

It's good to be in Miami these days.

writing in the sun,
wading in the waters,
Waiting for life.

Bud Lights
and
been listening to a lot
of Franco Cotardo,
and Eric Schmidt, too.

Resting
in restlessness;
I just can't wait.

If I were to fall asleep
by the pool...

I'd drown.

Where People Are Lions

We are burping artists,
nostalgic for a time that never existed,
never wearing shoes without socks.

I am drinking vodka straight from the bottle,
and feeling sorry for myself.

This is a Fun Monday, indeed,
with a capitol F-U.

Favorite Probably Laughter

mechanical pencils
along with the radio
and
my favorite dive bar.

I still call stars nicks
in the glass sky,
sparks in the making.

I ramble like the Rumbler,
only above ground.

I stand up and dance
for five minutes
and then sit back down in chairs,
uncomfortable and comfortable.

I see the moon,
and my wrists hurt,
because they need bracelets,
always as always
as humans need love,
wrapped around them forever
or for now.

There's a chance at
garbage bags
and pissing in a waste of living,
while loving loud
and blowing out birthday candles.

something else

inside
the [cage] that we all love
and sell and sing
and laugh
along New Orleans.

the ceilings were too tall.
our hearts were a quarter to twelve.

part two is part two
in the history of things
and birds.

Pots

This is dumb.
Lowercase Laughter.
Guitar my restarted retarded heart.

Laugh your way this way
and change my mind
into fossils.

Save me tonight
in pots with pans.

Find Me Kill

and thus the faith begins
like black holes
dense and floating in some river
of outer space,
and beautiful girls
with side-boobs exposed
like never before
in my backyard.

This is my life,
and I write it.

I hurt my back
trying
to map oblivion
for you fit
so lift us up.

Surroundings

Let's make up poems
about love
and life,
and then just give up
and surrender to werds
misspelled,
and art
chopped up,
and let life pass us right by
like a motherfucker
on the street
with the sniffles
at breakneck speed,
tying up your hands.

Goddamn it!
You know what I mean,
as we walk down change blvd.
and voices voice voices and translations.

90 Ounces to Poverty

Meat Scraps, indeed.
Want to go to Poland?
Or Portland?
Maine or Oregon?
Kayle chips.
And be the daughter of a man.
Who is a mammal.
Like the rest of us?

Sounds sexy for a rodent.
We can't afford anything.
So we chose a sight,
because it's free
for now.

Okay, I am being either a good time
or ridiculous.

Firecracker

I barely knew her,
so I will make this poem up...

I do know that we hooked up
on a warm night
after the Penrose
in her peach sheets,
maybe they were red.

Thunder,
lightning broke my heart ,
and all I got was this lousy t-shirt.

Then there was Rhyming poetry
and sparklers.

Sometimes I call her cold,
but I never call her Francis anymore.
Sometimes I drunk dial her.
Bold, but I never...

Your Frown's Up!

put this summer
behind peacock backs,
this year is almost over.

say the sentences,
but don't ever speak,
tomorrow is not good for silver tears.

a see-saw,
and some somersaults,
I can't wait for the cardigan cold.

the stars upon wonderful shoulders,
sing me asleep,
grow denser and lovelier during the railroad nights.

colors seem longer, too.
I race to the top of the hill,
just to look down.

Where is Boiceville, NY?

past the sleeve and the stripe.
past the empty chair.
past the empty sky.
grey days seem green and seamless.

past the red ropes and the bronze lantern.
past the hills and the house.
past the sage and the flagless flagpole.
you've been famous since your birth.

past the trees and the footbridge.
past the firewood and the joke for a toolshed.
past the parking lot and the river.
listen to the math.

Mountain Fire

she keeps mountain fire
and sings along
with me
while
I am doing my best
to save the world.

tell me the names
of the poems
I am in,
said the day, suffer.

throw a shell back into the sea.
and play and run
gather up the nights.

she kept morning fire, too.
she is smarter than you.

cats run in the background
and clue in me
to the wish lists.

the day won't leave me alone.
to do this as alleyway songs
are not allowed.

dust off your angry shoes outside.
empty your soul in an empty room.
get stuck between my teeth.

Admirable Work, Boyo

who is scared in the
American wing of the MET?

while wearing a grey suit...

competing patterns
of gin
with the versatility of a truck,
want to fix this?

it's about to be that blue time
that I like so much.

the floor is uptown, too.

I swear I am good now.

the subject matter is lost.
I am a sea of plots.
maybe colours.

gunshots

I remember every time
I kissed your neck.

You loved that the best.

while dreaming,
darling,
I start shooting
at coffee cups.

let's jump out
the window
and go back in time.

tigers and hurricanes
still exist
somewhere.
love exists, too.

Thanks, Mud

indeed,
I write poetry to shut your eyes,
and to get you to sigh
in country disbelief.

bullshit,
my ankles
write poetry, too (first poem),
better than my fingers.

curiosity is not a luxury.

I am a noble animal,
and I can hear your heart beating
from the hill.

join me for a lung.
godspeed.
goddamn this year.
snow prints
swarm foreign in some diner.

I want to work on a train.
don't let men eat our house.

Past-Tense Pretend

You were a perfect brunette
from the Midwest,
wild
without tattoos.

In ugly clothes,
you are gorgeous,
and naked
and young
and demented.

Call me yours.
Call me always.
Call me tall.

The Goat Series, Part One

this is my Goat Series,
called Judith, formally.

I do not have any obligations.

you know what's funny?
chicks yawning!

got the tables
and
my teeth are white
and
they get licked.

if I have found mercy,
surely you can, too.
the world makes
a five dollar difference.

you don't know how life feels.

owls are amazing.
And I can see the train tracks
out the bathroom window.

widow piss
and pentode lies.

be mine all of the time.

Sharp Hips and Funky Eyebrows

For the future,
the song stops,
and then keeps going.

Cool for sure,
and always important,
and impatient,
as I.

Fuck Eric.
And fuck Angels!
And fuck breaking down boxes.
And fuck restaurant stairs.

I will come back half alive
without telephones
or hills.

Come into my kitchen for an ugly cry,
and have breakfast with billionaires.
Tell me to shower!
And come to eventually see the please.

Logorrhea

In the vein of hills and clouds,
can we start something new from the ground?

I will return in a seaplane
amidst the peach porch forest.

I'll talk to the cousins
about horizons and hands;
my choices are waterfalls.

The steeples are downstairs,
and the placemats are nineteen orange,
but the weight of the world right now
is somehow eight pounds less.

Poem

desperate, low-life autumn eyes,
blue at times, brown at night;
I spell your name in the snow
with blood from ripped stitches.

knit a road to a map;
glue stain a map to your busted heart,
and sew a secret kiss to a vest.
and so a secret kiss sets me adrift.

hope hurts and the moon is on fire.
let's live out our lives,
rich and wrecked,
until they wheel out the caskets of dash.

okay you win,
so devilishly sexy with sun off the haunted
road.

Orlando (fucking) Florida

my demons walk with me
in soft songs;
they told me not to leave them.

my feet were swept off the muddy slate
just off of Church Street.
while
I remember the old house
on Alcock Street.

everyone was burning roofing
shingles in the backyard
with Steve and Mom,
and I had to go to the hospital:
Asthma attack.

my sister had a husband once upon a time.
she got real sick
right after I moved away.
she raised me.
she is my Mom.
we never talked about how
our real mother dear
had nothing to say.

Heather's father raised her.

I made a mess,
but it's okay.

First thought, best thought.
Last thought, worst thought.

The weather was unkind.
It rained every single fucking day.

Back then.

a poem that will hopefully punch your throat so hard you will die happy

white batteries.
cold catalogs.
I find my hope here without fire nights.
and shadow eyeballs.
on the edge of your forest.
this is the place where teachers disappear.
ferns grow invisible.
brown grows black.
and guesses grow grey.
for things like ladies.
forgotten frog friends live in sandwiches.
and I am late for work, all the time.
if. if. if. if. if. if. if. if. if.
you are a century cliff-hanger.
I don't know a good goddamn salad day.
your thing captures my thing.
the backyard is now west and full of mudbugs.
attention is careful.
I keep my eyes on you.
you watch your way.
street toes and cacti.
withering wi-fi.
I am still a fool.
so are you.
thirsty.
white batteries.
cold catalogs. indeed.
become your own favorite.

The First Day of Last Year's Autumn
was September 22nd

This is last year,
or the year before;
oh! who the fuck cares,
the day after birthdays...
I'm glad you were borne unto this.

no answer to the call of the *if*,
and to the seasons that drift
in and out of our kitchens,
so we celebrate two days,
maybe thirty,
given the chance.

what happened to the nothing
that we preached upon motorbikes?
this is New York...
each block is different.

come walking
down the street.
sometimes friends are me...
leave the facts on the corner.

we will figure out the fragrances of the future,
and which ones surround the sounds
of your neck like a noose called *next*.

hope is a currency.

water is wet.
the sky is blue.

life is good,
and worth living.

It's Easy

It's easy arson fights in rivers.
Pretty said she prayed today.
gin girls go away.
I'll never be great.
misunderstood pink punk rock.
like this.

Easy Shit.
splash the bracelet across your wrist.
be camouflaged and caliber valiant.

here's a *There* and a *Q* needle.
at the bottom of a talkative bottom night.
lose the rain.
chew names like guesses and Clint Eastwood.
it's okay to shoot the past that's annoying you.

It's easy to be the back of the knees instead of the
front.
please them their bending notions.
every day is just a dream stuck inside a machine gun.

only one ear works, I spy Buddha and a beast.
no need for violence.
day is constantly breaking, hearts are waking,
overheard.
It's easy when there are more people out there to love
than who love you.

Sweet Dreams, Kendra Jean

The eyes of her have
cut the mundane middle of this world
like nothing this place has ever scene,
while folk songs play and pry into my life,
thus lacking the disappearing affect
of my teeth and my smoked-out garden;
my hands are good at making.

Everything and nothing and everything
from the falling sky
to her shoelaces
reminds me of the days we will miss.

Bliss and bullshit behind bartenders' backs.

Close those eyes to the world
and dream seamless dreams, please:
rivers in the middle of train tracks,
taking canoes and trains to my heart and ears.

I want to see you sleep and dream,
only to see you wake
with those big beautiful eyes,
like lightbrown heavenly light.

Tonight, please have sweet seamless dreams
and, in them,
be with me.

Let Us Map Oblivion

we burned all our clothes,
blew yak up our noses.
young and crazy,
we were borne this week,
dead and unique.

we stood on the platform in vain.
we sat on a crackhead bench in Union Sq.

maybe we are bricks and mortar now,
running down nights,
trying to map oblivion.

I would bet one or two of us
will be dead by the next decade.

Hay Machine

the wind collects old scarecrows
and puts them all on the roof of the barn.
Shoshana has stopped singing.
and Tedder started hearing gossip.
the morning rag predicts the end
and always allows us to have the
high school football scores.
the field was good to us this spring
and summer.
The rusty maker is still going strong
in that old shed, the eastern one,
that wayward ghosts built a century ago.
we caught some shrimp;
threw some furniture down the hill
near the common creek.
the windmill broke in an argument with said wind.

And you don't have to worry about before.
Sincerely, Yours.

Style, Stance, Song

small steps in paper bags,
arms covered in alarms,
how come
this is how it [always] goes?

find yourself
trembling between fireworks,
so sweet
it might make you behave
or believe.

small steps in questions marks,
arms covered in songs,
eyelids [always] begging to open
tomorrow.

Comma Vomit

I wasn't sure what this month would bring...

but it brought the business, a sliced pinky,
and lots of sweat, bad cliches,
and wastes of time,
extinction and big colours.

for the time being,
time being time being time,
I play the simple accordion,
light a cigarette,
look for slick sick black socks,
and beg the sambo not to put nickels on my eyes.

as I lay my head down,
skies should be clear of hard hearts,
and I know movies,
and I heard the final clapping song in a
dream.

sitting and being me
as best I can,
nodding to strangers without umbrellas,
I'm thoroughly enjoying the midnight rain,
for windmill once, for war,
and for tomorrow,
for all.

I'm Robbing a Bank,
Can I Call Ya' Right Back?

I sing with passions, these silly songs you call poems.
I call them mine.
They are my only weapons.
and I use them to rob a bank.

Short, little, sharp sentences.
That cut palindromes and moms.
I let a rabbit go in the lobby.
And I call my dead ma' collect from jail.

Hopefully,
one dead day,
I will be a folk hero
in Kansas or Kentucky.

Paper Gator

in twenty-seven days
and twenty odd hours
I will become a paper alligator,
and my heart will be in a plastic bag.
I need you to need me tonight.

take to the talking bridge.

wish over it
when the numbers match,
way west with empty.

in ten years,
these months won't matter.
those days will.
these moments will taste like anger,
but when the river pulse runs the veins with rakes,
we will smell something familiar
and shake at an airport desk.

let's get ugly and strong,
reptilian, ghost.
long way now,
the devil's in our old town,
two stops short of Babylon.

I felt the cut.
between fingers.
you said you would.
and you did.

wear the newspaper.
make it through the night,
burn in the fire.

we will save each other in a swamp.
or a factory.
or a river city.
or a pub.
fucked up
in ten years
when the paper has yellowed and time has won.

Don't Be Like The Rest
of Them, Darling

dear Portland, please stop by my eye spy.
be a murder mystery with a happy ending.

outside,
you've been searching for something you'll never find...

heavy is the head that gets no sleep,
plus the apathy.
we carry our lives around
in our memories.

...so stop searching, just be.

We are the best explorers, celebrations happen.

Xip

Somewhere
we go
to kill
the cup
and capture
the mountains
hiding north of royal,
or simply behind the package store.

I don't think I want to think about
summer time.

You knew *I* was gonna happen,
didn't you?

awful little thieves

in the night
run
I need a reason to kick
you.

shins and chins
bad habits
claws
part two.

I don't care about your white wooden pears.
collar bones are awful little thieves.
stealing my rapid heartbeats.

I will win.
after I've lost.
my shoulders will leave for the stars.
but I will still.
be here.
even if I am.
there.

The Ravine

ironic wolves in the orchard west,
you can tell where we are by the trees.
I hear them all
and
two rivers east.

walking
with
wild sunflowers,
my feet stink so I throw away my socks,
hoping I will see a deer with them on later antlers.

trucks took us here,
me and a fishing pole and a nasty little notebook.
I read poetry to the prayer mountains,
whole while trout fishing
for the first time in this last life.
two rivers converge, stories down,
created by an ice age,
I have never been to this square inch
before.
I liked history class in middle school,
but I still don't know what that
means: *created by.*
yet, here I stand
in this square inch of my own history,
fishing for wild
just north of imagination,
grey hairs in my mustache,
none on my head, thankful.

with wild sunflowers, early June,
ancient in every way
except me and the otters;
my cellular telephone doesn't work and dies
a thousand and two times,
like me.

Pretty, Great

lots of notes
left
lots of smiles
lots of beers
good
this is the breeze .

see the action
meet me in Tukwila, WA
for dive-bar poetics.

be big on this raucous surface
be titles & waves.

take risks out to lunch.

Philosophy and a Haircut

I go to a girl called Irena.
She has been cutting my hair since I cut the long hair
all off.
She knows exactly how I like it;
she doesn't even need to ask anymore.
There is something comforting in that respect.
And her volatile voice.
She is a talker, though,
and she is deep,
gabbing and lecturing on the circles and cycles of the
souls of the world.
She came from Russia, studied Kabala.
She makes me feel bad,
because I just get high and write.
No peace of mind.
But I listen long and hard.
It's just a typical Tuesday,
and I leave with existentialism and trimmed sideburns,
wondering how people get their haircut
and don't immediately take a shower immediately
after.
Itching chaos.
Itching life.
Wash it off sometimes
and start a new circle and/or cycle.
Skeletons don't need haircuts.

don't know Always.

things ever happen...
my eyes are shaped like snakes.
I throw boats.
hold the happenings.
I am the worst person I know.
something of love.
mountains look like mountains.
ant hills look like ant hills.
life is relative to the size of our eyes.
ac·cou·tre·ment.
watching weekends and helicopters combined.
reverse my hands.
pretend for pretending's sake.
like a spiral staircase.
trying to be orange and new.
surprise!
It's old and grey.
I am not a kite at night.
Crayola me.
trouble is a vision.
it takes someone to get back.
it takes scary to see.
be the sea's dream of land.
as only motion pictures can paint with fright.
wait until you hold it.
life like wind.
tough to put in a heart bag.
claim.
steal.
as you get older, you get older.

everyone must be everyone.
and decide for themselves.
like the lonely kazoo.
to annoy silence.
eighteen percent of wrong is right.
ears get cold.
warm throat.
I can't believe people live in places like Cleveland and
Houston and Jacksonville.
what do they do there?
just being neighbors must suck.
this here song, I try to sing.
bracelets get dirty like knees.
tell me goodnight with your lovely voice.
I want to be a stick figure.
in someone else's drawing on a bar napkin.

This is the DNA of odd Love...

Capone

chains,
and I heard a violin...

combat,
this day will die with tomorrow...

eulogized as yesterland.

you gotta do what you're meant to do,
what you want to get out of life:

tigers
and
new days.

Nothing in the Background

bloom like bonus tracks,
train like locomotives,
motivate like mornings filled with possibilities.
write me a letter,
and fill my impatient head with pieces,
of the You.

pull the sun down,
sleep close when far.

count the hats,
give them hands.

and purple oval headaches
give me a name
and fight travel with a dull Civil War sword.

be a video,
be a game.

save your six dollars
for the store and river wishes
sparks in the dark.

wake up to the sound of your fleeting
a hedge maze,
woods land,
stuck 'til dead.

be a scrape on my funny bone.

make me laugh and think about blood.

play all we play,
listen to slow songs loud,
while doing the goddamn dishes.

break a mug out of spite for that mug's history of tea.

don't stop running until you reach the one
and the sun.

let the meter run out.
quarters are still there.

be cold and hot and horny and not.

be a flood.
(how little you know.)
be a window, not a wall.
stand at the foot of a bed.
stand at the foot of a path.
look both ways before crossing the street.
sleep to rest, sleep to dream.
find the years, find them yet.
fight them.

be there.
see slow.
and always know always and always know how to dare
life to eyes.

Saxophone Bologna Sandwich

I bite my nails on the bridge,
spitting the clippings over the edge.
I pen a poem without a name.
I name a limerick after you.

I want to be young
(in a better Brooklyn),
I want to be the little spoon
(in a bedroom).

Seventeen minutes is forever
especially
in new hawks,
kneeling,
seeing lovely legs,
in a skinny jeans symphony,
and I eat sad pizza.

also,
I see Kyle walking up the street,
shorts and flip-flops,
telling me to be better.

crash! Ghost.
hallucinations are like this.
rewarding. Resonating.
when I got the music,
I got a place to go.

We Made it to the Coastline

Signs,
a different serene,
watch the road.

Soundtracks,
folk hero, doubtless.

these days
it's a sin to not like Radiohead.
I am a sea-sewn sinner.

hearts are works of art.
who is the artist?
you or you or a ewe or her again or Hashem.

we made it to the coin-toss coast.
Heads or Tales.

pick a snack from a mulberry bush.
some other time
is always on my mind.

cover it slow.
I'll see ya at the folk show.

just give up on the land.
And my hands.

yeah, there's an undertow,
but it ain't got me.

waiting on a hot air balloon.
you should pen a poem all over this.

So I did,
a fire started by old bills,
brought with
a bottle of Knob Creek.

And,
the trouble with coastlines is that one can see forever.
grace is neither time nor place dependent.
you will have blood on your hands.
always. armor.
tis not all in vain.

By Death, Danger, and Love

Like a saloonkeeper,
my palms sweat with the worst of them
and by glory being bullshit;
what a place to start this synthesis in Brooklyn,
where love fell
and I still eat treason.

Who needs to fall?
I certainly don't,
unless it is Autumn in this half-hour town.

Mix Tape 9 & How to Materialize

2. *Two Kids* by Strand of Oaks
3. *Year of the Cat* by The Lemonheads
4. *Caution* by Foreign Talks
5. *Ballad of Larry Bird* by Vermont
6. *Ray* by Millencollin
7. *Monsters with Misdemeanors* by Yellow Red Sparks
8. *Ty Cobb* by Soundgarden
9. *I Don't Want To Set The World on Fire* by The Ink Spots

*worry about #1 and #10!

Poem

I feel young.
again.
the end.

www.ingramcontent.com/pod-product-compliance
Lightning Source LLC
LaVergne TN
LVHW051545080426
835510LV00020B/2857